LET'S
see

Unusual Farms

by Brenda Haugen

Content Adviser: Susan Thompson, Agriculture Communications,
College of Agriculture, Iowa State University

Reading Adviser: Susan Kesselring, M.A., Literacy Educator,
Rosemount-Apple Valley-Eagan (Minnesota) School District

Let's See Library
Compass Point Books
Minneapolis, Minnesota

To my sister Tammy Iwen and my brother, Jamie Haugen, who haven't strayed too far from the North Dakota farm on which we grew up. I love you both! BH

Compass Point Books
3109 West 50th Street, #115
Minneapolis, MN 55410

Visit Compass Point Books on the Internet at *www.compasspointbooks.com*
or e-mail your request to *custserv@compasspointbooks.com*

On the cover: An adult male ostrich with baby ostriches

Photographs ©: Adam Jones/Visuals Unlimited, cover; Keren Su/Corbis, 4; Hans Georg Roth/Corbis, 6; Layne Kennedy/Corbis, 8; Minden Pictures/Larry Minden, 10; U.S. Department of Agriculture/Ken Hammond, 12; Charles & Josette Lenars/Corbis, 14; Corbis, 16; Stuart Westmorland/Corbis, 18; Image Ideas, 20.

Creative Director: Terri Foley
Managing Editor: Catherine Neitge
Editor: Brenda Haugen
Photo Researcher: Marcie C. Spence
Designers: Melissa Kes and Jaime Martens
Educational Consultant: Diane Smolinski

Library of Congress Cataloging-in-Publication Data
Haugen, Brenda.
  Unusual farms / by Brenda Haugen.
      p. cm. — (Let's see)
Includes index.
ISBN 0-7565-0668-9 (hardcover)
  1.Farms—Juvenile literature. 2. Agriculture—Juvenile literature. I. Title. II. Series.
S519.H379 2005
  630—dc22   2004005560

Table of Contents

NOTE: In this book, words that are defined in the glossary
are in **bold** the first time they appear in the text.

4

What Is Found on Unusual Farms?

A sign for an ostrich farm stands along a quiet highway in North Dakota. Farther up the road, bison roam in a **pasture.** Near Seattle, Washington, some farmers raise giant grass called **bamboo.** In China, silkworm farmers collect fine thread that will be made into pretty cloth.

These might not be the kinds of animals and plants you would expect to see on a farm. There are unusual farms all around the world, however. Some grow unusual plants. Some raise unusual animals. Still others make something you can't even see! Let's take a little trip and see what wonders we can find.

◄ *A worker takes care of silkworms on a silkworm farm in China.*

Ostrich Farms

Ostrich farms are found in many places around the world. Farmers raise these birds for their meat, eggs, feathers, and skin. Ostrich skin is used to make gloves, wallets, and boots.

Ostriches can run up to 40 miles (64 kilometers) per hour, but they cannot fly. Fences keep these birds from escaping.

Adult male ostriches are bigger than females. A male weighs about 350 pounds (158 kilograms) and stands around 8 feet (2.4 meters) tall.

Ostriches will eat lots of things, such as grass, bugs, and frogs. Ostriches on farms also may eat hay and fruit.

◄ *An ostrich and its young are fed at a farm in South Africa.*

Bison Ranches

About 300,000 bison, which also are called buffalo, live on ranches in the United States and Canada.

A male bison is called a bull. Bulls are bigger than female bison, which are called cows. Bulls can be 6 feet (1.8 meters) tall at the humps on their backs. These animals can weigh more than 2,000 pounds (900 kilograms).

Bison mainly eat grass, hay, and other plants. Ranchers put bison in pastures. These grassy areas have fences all around, so the bison don't run away.

These large animals are raised mainly for their meat. Their skins can be made into many things, including shoes, bags, and blankets.

◄ *Bison eat hay on the 777 Ranch in Hermosa, South Dakota.*

Llama Farms

In South America, llamas have been used to carry heavy loads for thousands of years. Today, llama farms can be found all around the world.

An adult llama weighs about 400 pounds (180 kilograms) and can be 6 feet (1.8 meters) tall. Llamas eat grass, oats, and hay. They also need shelter from heat and rain.

A llama's wool, or hair, is thick and long. The wool can be made into sweaters and blankets. Llamas make good pets, but farmers still raise them to carry loads, too. A llama can carry as much as 130 pounds (59 kilograms). A llama that thinks its load is too heavy may refuse to move!

◄ *A girl leads a llama in California. Llamas are related to camels, but have no humps.*

Fish Farms

Farmers raise fish for many reasons. Some raise fish for people to eat. Others sell **fingerlings** to people who want to put fish in their own ponds. Other farmers may raise small fish that will be used as bait by fishermen.

Some fish farms have many ponds. Other fish farms may be sections of a river or ocean that have been closed off with nets. Fish farms can even be large water tanks inside buildings.

Different fish eat different kinds of food. They may eat worms or **algae.** Farmers may feed fish special pellets that help them grow. The faster the fish grow, the faster the farmers can sell them.

◀ *Workers harvest catfish from a farm in Mississippi.*

Silkworm Farms

Silk is made by caterpillars called silkworms.
Silk cloth can be made into clothes and curtains.

Many silkworm farms are in China and Japan.
Farmers feed silkworms **mulberry** leaves to help
them grow. When silkworms are fully grown, they
make **cocoons.** Each silkworm builds a cocoon in its
little space in a cardboard frame. Each cocoon is
made of one tightly wound strand of silk that is
more than one mile (1.6 kilometers) long.

Farmers put the cocoons in hot ovens. This kills
the silkworms. Then the cocoons are sent to
factories where the silk thread is unwound.

◄ *Cocoons are sorted at a silkworm farm in China.*

Tree Farms

Wood from trees is used to make lots of **products.** Many houses are made from wood. It is used to make paper and some kinds of pencils, too.

There are more than 65,000 tree farms in the United States.

Tree farmers might sell trees to make products people use. They may sell trees to people who want to plant them in their own yards. Some grow Christmas trees for people to enjoy in their homes.

Farmers replace the trees they sell by planting new trees. That way, there will always be more trees in the future.

◄ *Trees growing on a farm*

Bamboo Farms

Bamboo is a tall grass that can grow quickly. Some bamboo can grow 3 feet (90 centimeters) in one day!

Bamboo may be 1 foot (30 centimeters) to more than 100 feet (30.5 meters) tall. It grows mainly in warm, wet places.

On farms, bamboo grows in **groves.** Farmers may put hard concrete underground. The concrete keeps the bamboo's roots from spreading.

Bamboo's strong, woody stems can be made into chairs, fences, fishing poles, flutes, baskets, and much more. The small, young bamboo shoots can even be eaten!

◄ *Bamboo plants grow in Hawaii where the weather is warm and moist.*

Wind Farms

Some farmers work with something that isn't living at all. They work with wind.

Many wind farms are found on flat, open lands or in the ocean where the wind is strong. On these farms, wind turns big, tall **turbines** or windmills that are used to make electricity. Denmark was the first country to use wind energy in this way.

Energy from wind farms is used in homes—maybe to cook bison burgers! Wind energy powers lights that let people read books at night. The paper in those books might have come from tree farms. The farms we visited may be unusual, but we use things from them every day.

◀ *Wind turbines on a wind farm*

Glossary

algae—tiny plants that live in water

bamboo—a grass with hard, hollow stems

cocoons—protective cases where insects or other animals develop before they hatch

fingerlings—baby fish that are between 2 and 4 inches (5 and 10 centimeters) long

groves—groups of trees or bamboo growing near one another

mulberry—a tree that has purple berries

pasture—a large field where animals can eat grass

products—things that are made or manufactured

turbines—engines driven by wind; the wind passes through long blades that spin in a circle and make the engine work

Did You Know?

• The ostrich is the only bird that has just two toes on each foot. Its hard, sharp toes and long, strong legs help an ostrich run very fast. In South Africa, people even ride ostriches in races! Riders steer the birds by pulling on their wings.

• On some fish farms there are many ponds. Each pond may be filled with a different kind of fish.

• When a llama is upset, it spits—usually at other llamas. The spit smells really bad, so the llama's enemies will probably learn to leave it alone if they ever get spit on.

• The largest bamboo plant reported in the United States was 70 feet (21 meters) tall. That's about as tall as seven elephants stacked on top of one another!

• Silk moths only live for two or three days. They have no mouths, so they can't eat. Their only job is to make babies. On silkworm farms, some silkworms are allowed to grow into silk moths and have young, so there are always more silkworms.

• When bison are born, they are orange. They turn brownish black as they get older. Wooly hair on the front of bison protects them from harsh winter storms.

Want to Know More?

In the Library

Blackaby, Susan. *The World's Largest Plants: A Book About Trees.* Minneapolis: Picture Window Books, 2003.

Crewe, Sabina. *The Buffalo.* Austin, Texas: Raintree Steck-Vaughn, 1998.

Heinrichs, Ann. *Fish.* Minneapolis: Compass Point Books, 2003.

Jacobs, Liza. *Silkworms.* San Diego: Blackbirch Press, 2003.

On the Web

For more information on *unusual farms,* use FactHound to track down Web sites related to this book.

1. Go to *www.facthound.com*
2. Type in a search word related to this book or this book ID: 0756506689.
3. Click on the *Fetch It* button.

Your trusty FactHound will fetch the best Web sites for you!

On the Road

Paradico Buffalo Farm and Resort
3456 State Highway 310
Norwood, NY 13668
315/384-8951
To take a wagon ride through a buffalo herd and visit a petting zoo

The Bullfrog Fish Farm
N1321 Bullfrog Road
Menomonie, WI 54751
715/664-8775
To see a working fish farm and go fishing

Index

About the Author

A graduate of the University of North Dakota in Grand Forks, Brenda Haugen is the author of several children's books. A writer and editor, Brenda is "Mom" to RaeLynn and Tylor and the family's four bunnies, and "Godmom" to Nicole. Brenda's funniest experience growing up on a farm was riding sideways on a horse as her sister Tammy, who was riding behind her, started to fall off.